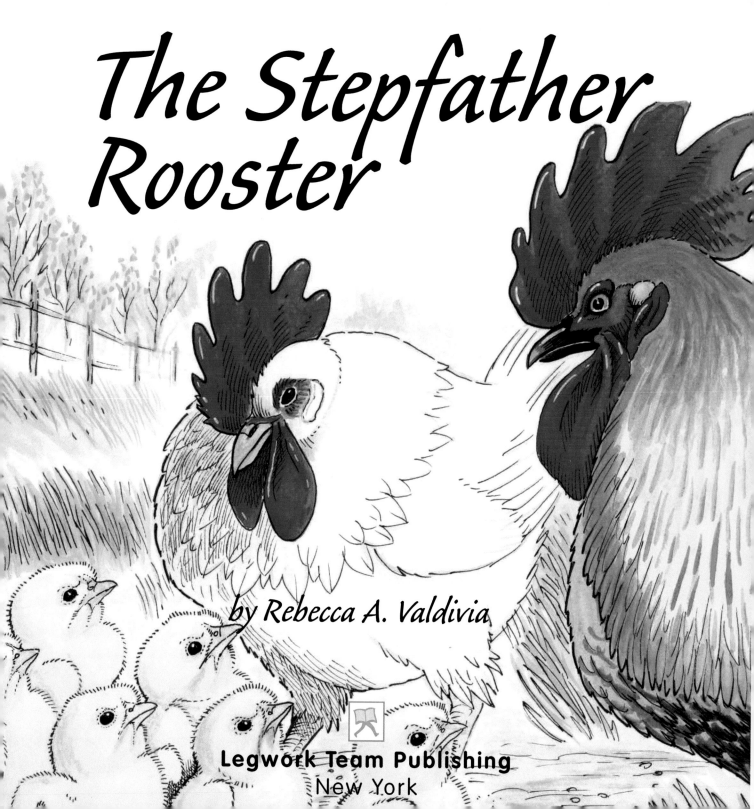

The Stepfather Rooster

by Rebecca A. Valdivia

Legwork Team Publishing
New York

AuthorHouse™
1663 Liberty Drive
Bloomington, IN 47403
www.authorhouse.com
Phone: 833-262-8899

Because of the dynamic nature of the Internet, any web addresses or links contained in this book may have changed since publication and may no longer be valid. The views expressed in this work are solely those of the author and do not necessarily reflect the views of the publisher, and the publisher hereby disclaims any responsibility for them.

Any people depicted in stock imagery provided by Getty Images are models, and such images are being used for illustrative purposes only.
Certain stock imagery © Getty Images.

Coverdesign, interior layout, and print-ready file by LegworkTeam Publishing

Illustrated by Christopher Donovan

This book is printed on acid-free paper.

ISBN: 978-1-4343-9040-0 (sc)

Print information available on the last page.

Published by AuthorHouse 02/23/2021

authorHOUSE®

To my children, Frank, Richard and Philip,
who have given me the ultimate mother's experience.
I love you unconditionally.

To my parents, Richard and Cristina Valdivia,
who said they loved me and would always be there for me.
Fifty years later they still are, with my mom on earth
and my dad in heaven.

And to my granddaughters, Kayla and Alicia,
who are my little princesses and bright stars.
You are my joy and hope for the future.

*O*nce upon a time on a small apple ranch, there lived a hen and a rooster. Jen the hen and Booster the rooster loved to strut around their chicken coop and peck at the ground for bugs. They especially loved it when Farmer Brown and his wife picked corn and let their children husk it, because they picked off the fat, juicy, delicious worms and fed them to Jen and Booster.

Farmer Brown and his wife, Mrs. Brown, had three little sons named Jimmy, Tommy and Pat. Jimmy was the oldest; he was sociable and very talkative. Tommy was very active and occasionally mischievous. Pat was the youngest and very quiet. The three brothers loved to play outside together.

8

Sometimes, on sunny afternoons, the boys opened the chicken coop door and let Jen and Booster out to wander for a while. They explored the soft earth of the apple orchard, and noticed other chickens next door at their neighbor's house.

One spring morning, Jen laid six brown eggs. After that, Jimmy, Tommy and Pat went to the chicken coop and peeked every day to see if the eggs had hatched. Jen sat and sat on her eggs each day and didn't want to go out in the yard anymore.

Booster started to get bored. One day Booster was so bored, he wandered off to the neighbor's house, where he met other chickens and roosters. He had so much fun that he decided to stay and live there. Jen became sad and lonely. She missed Booster very much.

The day finally arrived when Jen's eggs hatched. Now she had six little baby chicks to look after. She named them Chirpy, Fluffy, Peeper, Tuffy, Chip and Chancie. The boys were excited. Jimmy said, "Welcome to the world, little chickies! Glad to meet you!" Tommy peeked in the chicken coop and shouted, "Come out and play!" Pat just smiled and nodded. They let Jen and her chicks out of the chicken coop to go out and explore.

Jen loved her baby chicks, but she still missed Booster. One day, she decided to go to the neighbor's yard to look for him. She didn't see him, but something strange happened: she met another rooster! His name was Al. He was very kind to Jen and said he would go to live with her if she wanted. "Al, I have six baby chicks," Jen said. Al answered, "That's okay."

17

18

So Al went back to the chicken coop with Jen and became her new husband. That meant he was the stepfather to Jen's six baby chicks. At first the chicks did not like Al. "Who is this rooster, mother?" said Chirpy. Jen replied, "This is Al. He is to be your stepfather." The chicks felt confused. "He can't tell us what to do. He's not our dad," said Tuffy.

Time went by and the baby chicks grew. They were no longer babies. They were more like teenagers, about thirteen years old in human years. Al was very happy living with Jen and her chicks. Jen tried to be happy, but she still thought about Booster. One day, she went to go look for him.

21

The next morning, Al woke up and thought, "Hmmm, where is Jen?" He waited all day for her to come back. He waited days and weeks, and still she didn't return. Pretty soon the chicks started to ask Al, "Where is our mother?" And even though Al was worried, he calmly responded, "I don't know, but I'm sure she's okay. I'm here if you need me."

Well, Jen never came back. Can you believe that? She had walked so far, far away from home that she got lost and could not find her way back. She cried because she missed her chicks. One day Farmer Brown and his family were out in the yard working and doing chores. The boys decided to let the chicks and Al out of the chicken coop because it was such a nice, sunny afternoon.

25

All of a sudden, a huge hawk swooped down from out of nowhere and grabbed one of the chicks. It was Tuffy. Luckily, the hawk couldn't quite get away because Tuffy was struggling and thrashing about.

Then, before you knew it, Al was there, pecking and fighting with the hawk to let Tuffy loose. The hawk flapped its wings and tried to pull away, but Al flapped his wings, too, and pecked and pecked at the hawk's face and legs. Finally, the hawk got tired and gave up. He let go and dropped the chick.

Tuffy had a few bumps and scratches, but he was okay. He was crying and very scared, but he was also very glad he was alive. He looked up and said, "Thank you, Al. You saved my life! I love you very much." And Al the stepfather rooster hugged him and replied, "I love you, too."

Far away at another farm, Jen had found a new home. She still missed her chicks and thought of them every day, but she was happy because she knew Al the stepfather rooster would always take care of them.

About the Author

REBECCA A. VALDIVIA was born and raised in Watsonville, California. She attended Notre Dame High School in Salinas, CA, Cabrillo Community College in Aptos, CA and California State University in Fresno, CA. She has worked for twenty years in education and has volunteered with the Family Partnership Program of Children's Mental Health, ToughLove, and the Migrant Education RIF Program. She has been published in the Fall, 1990 issue of "Poetic Voices of America" as well as in "El Andar" newspaper, 1989-1990, in Watsonville, CA.

Purchase Information Page

Copies of this book may be purchased through

AuthorHouse.com, BarnesAndNoble.com,

Borders.com, and Amazon.com.

You can also obtain a copy by ordering it

from your favorite book store.